D0845333

SandCastle 3

Homophones

Do We By, Buy, or Bye Tickets?

Amanda Rondeau

ABDO
Publishing Company

Published by SandCastle™, an imprint of ABDO Publishing Company, 4940 Viking Drive, Edina, Minnesota 55435.

Copyright © 2002 by Abdo Consulting Group, Inc. International copyrights reserved in all countries. No part of this book may be reproduced in any form without written permission from the publisher. SandCastle™ is a trademark and logo of ABDO Publishing Company. Printed in the United States.

Cover and interior photo credits: Corbis Images, Eyewire Images, PhotoDisc, Rubberball Productions

Library of Congress Cataloging-in-Publication Data

Rondeau, Amanda, 1974-
    Do we by, buy, or bye tickets? / Amanda Rondeau.
      p. cm. -- (Homophones)
    Includes index.
    Summary: Photographs and simple text introduce homophones, words that sound alike but are spelled differently and have different meanings.
    ISBN 1-57765-782-9
    1. English language--Homonyms--Juvenile literature. [1. English language--Homonyms.] I. Title. II. Series.

PE1595 .R68 2002
428.1--dc21

                                                                        2001053373

The SandCastle concept, content, and reading method have been reviewed and approved by a national advisory board including literacy specialists, librarians, elementary school teachers, early childhood education professionals, and parents.

Let Us Know

After reading the book, SandCastle would like you to tell us your stories about reading. What is your favorite page? Was there something hard that you needed help with? Share the ups and downs of learning to read. We want to hear from you! To get posted on the ABDO Publishing Company Web site, send us email at:

sandcastle@abdopub.com

About SandCastle™

Nonfiction books for the beginning reader

- Basic concepts of phonics are incorporated with integrated language methods of reading instruction. Most words are short, and phrases, letter sounds, and word sounds are repeated.

- Book levels are based on the ATOS™ for Books formula. Other considerations for readability include the number of words in each sentence, the number of characters in each word, and word lists based on curriculum frameworks.

- Full-color photography reinforces word meanings and concepts.

- "Words I Can Read" list at the end of each book teaches basic elements of grammar, helps the reader recognize the words in the text, and builds vocabulary.

- Reading levels are indicated by the number of flags on the castle.

SandCastle uses the following definitions for this series:

- Homographs: words that are spelled the same but sound different and have different meanings. *Easy memory tip: "-graph"= same look*

- Homonyms: words that are spelled and sound the same but have different meanings. *Easy memory tip: "-nym"= same name*

- Homophones: words that sound alike but are spelled differently and have different meanings. *Easy memory tip: "-phone"= sound alike*

Look for more SandCastle books in these three reading levels:

Level 1 (one flag)	**Level 2** (two flags)	**Level 3** (three flags)

Grades Pre-K to K 5 or fewer words per page	**Grades K to 1** 5 to 10 words per page	**Grades 1 to 2** 10 to 15 words per page

Note: Some pages in this book contain more than 15 words in order to more clearly convey the concept of the book.

by
next to; through
the work or
means of; past

buy
to purchase
something

bye
short for
"good-bye"

Homophones are words that sound alike but are spelled differently and have different meanings.

I save money in my piggy bank.

I am saving up to buy a game.

I had to go home.

We said bye by the side of the road.

We like to buy ice cream when we go to the beach.

It tastes good.

Carrie is my best friend.

I hug her when we say bye.

He plays songs **by** many artists.

Ann likes to sing along.

Jenna is excited.

Her dad will buy her new hockey gear.

I say bye to my mom when I leave for school.

I like to sit **by** my sister when she reads to me.

We buy bread at the bakery.

They also sell cakes.

Joe is going on a trip.

He waved bye to his friends.

We went to a pumpkin patch and sat by the pumpkins in the field.

We buy pumpkins by the pound.

This one is heavy.

We wave bye to our mom in the morning.

She goes to work early.

I ride the bus after school and get off **by** my house.

The family drove by us in a white car.

They waved bye.

Eva shops with her mom.

What kind of fruit do they buy?

(oranges)

Words I Can Read

Nouns

A noun is a person, place, or thing

artists (AR-tistss) p. 10
bakery (BAYK-ur-ee)
  p. 14
beach (BEECH) p. 8
bread (BRED) p. 14
bus (BUHSS) p. 19
cakes (KAYKSS) p. 14
car (KAR) p. 20
dad (DAD) p. 11
family (FAM-uh-lee)
  p. 20
field (FEELD) p. 16
friend (FREND) p. 9
friends (FRENDZ) p. 15
fruit (FROOT) p. 21
game (GAME) p. 6
gear (GIHR) p. 11
hockey (HOK-ee) p. 11
home (HOME) p. 7

homophones
  (HOME-uh-fonez)
  p. 5
house (HOUSS) p. 19
ice cream (EYESS
  KREEM) p. 8
kind (KINDE) p. 21
meanings (MEE-ningz)
  p. 5
means (MEENZ) p. 4
mom (MOM)
  pp. 12, 18, 21
money (MUHN-ee) p. 6
morning (MOR-ning)
  p. 18
one (WUHN) p. 17
oranges (OR-inj-ez)
  p. 21
patch (PACH) p. 16

piggy bank
  (PIG-ee BANGK)
  p. 21
pound (POUND) p. 17
pumpkin (PUHMP-kin)
  p. 16
pumpkins
  (PUHMP-kinz)
  pp. 16, 17
road (ROHD) p. 7
school (SKOOL)
  pp. 12, 19
side (SIDE) p. 7
sister (SISS-tur) p. 13
songs (SAWNGZ) p. 10
trip (TRIP) p. 15
words (WURDZ) p. 5
work (WURK) pp. 4, 18

Proper Nouns

A proper noun is the name
of a person, place, or thing

Ann (AN) p. 10
Carrie (KA-ree) p. 9

Eva (EEV-uh) p. 21
Jenna (JEN-uh) p. 11

Joe (JOH) p. 15

22

Pronouns

A pronoun is a word that replaces a noun

he (HEE) pp. 10, 15

her (HUR) pp. 9, 11

I (EYE)
  pp. 6, 7, 9, 12, 13, 19

it (IT) p. 8

me (MEE) p. 13

she (SHEE) pp. 13, 18

something
  (SUHM-thing) p. 4

they (THAY)
  pp. 14, 20, 21

us (UHSS) p. 20

we (WEE)
  pp. 7, 8, 9, 14, 16, 17, 18

what (WUHT) p. 21

Verbs

A verb is an action or being word

am (AM) p. 6

are (AR) p. 5

buy (BYE)
  pp. 4, 6, 8, 11, 14, 17, 21

do (DOO) p. 21

drove (DROVE) p. 20

get (GET) p. 19

go (GOH) pp. 7, 8

goes (GOHZ) p. 18

going (GOH-ing) p. 15

had (HAD) p. 7

have (HAV) p. 5

hug (HUHG) p. 9

is (IZ) pp. 9, 11, 15, 17

leave (LEEV) p. 12

like (LIKE) pp. 8, 13

likes (LIKESS) p. 10

plays (PLAYZ) p. 10

purchase (PUR-chuhss)
  p. 4

reads (REEDZ) p. 13

ride (RIDE) p. 19

said (SED) p. 7

sat (SAT) p. 16

save (SAYV) p. 6

saving (SAYV-ing) p. 6

say (SAY) pp. 9, 12

sell (SEL) p. 14

shops (SHOPSS) p. 21

sing (SING) p. 10

sit (SIT) p. 13

sound (SOUND) p. 5

spelled (SPELD) p. 5

tastes (TAYSTSS) p. 8

wave (WAYV) p. 18

waved (WAYVD)
  pp. 15, 20

went (WENT) p. 16

will (WIL) p. 11

Adjectives

An adjective describes something

alike (uh-LIKE) p. 5
best (BEST) p. 9
different (DIF-ur-uhnt)
   p. 5
excited (ek-SITE-ed)
   p. 11
good (GUD) p. 8

heavy (HEV-ee) p. 17
her (HUR) p. 21
his (HIZ) p. 15
many (MEN-ee) p. 10
my (MYE)
   pp. 6, 9, 12, 13, 19
new (NOO) p. 11

our (OUR) p. 18
short (SHORT) p. 4
this (THISS) p. 17
white (WITE) p. 20

Adverbs

An adverb tells how, when, or where something happens

also (AWL-soh) p. 14

differently
   (DIF-ur-uhnt-lee) p. 5

early (UR-lee) p. 18
up (UHP) p. 6